Grapes

Apples

Pear

Avocado pears

Grapefruit

Orange

Satsuma

Grenadillo

Tamarillo

Limes

Lemon

D0996949

For Felicity and Clemmie
R.D.

For Katie, Liza, Jamie and Harriet
C.W.

The authors and publishers would like to thank
the following for their help in testing the recipes
in this book: Lucy Paynter; Classes 4D and 5H,
Middle Row Primary School, Kensal Rise, London W10;
the staff and pupils of Bousfield Primary School,
South Bolton Gardens, London SW5.

Text © 1993, 1996 Roz Denny and Caroline Waldegrave
Illustrations © 1993 Maureen Roffey, 1996 Jacky Paynter
Photographs © 1993 Hilary Moore, 1996 David Armstrong
Home Economists: Sandra Baddeley and Gina Steer
Stylists: Sue Russell and Suzy Gittins

First published as *The Walker Book of Children's Cookery* (2000)
by Walker Books Ltd
87 Vauxhall Walk, London SE11 5HJ

This edition published 2005
10 9 8 7 6 5 4 3 2 1

Printed in China

The book has been typeset in ITC Garamond

British Library Cataloguing in Publication Data:
a catalogue record for this book is
available from the British Library
ISBN: 1-4063-0277-5

THE
QUICK AND EASY
COOKBOOK
FOR KIDS

Roz Denny and
Caroline Waldegrave

WALKER BOOKS
AND SUBSIDIARIES
LONDON · BOSTON · SYDNEY · AUCKLAND

Contents

Authors' Note

We love cooking with our children (and their friends) and
have developed the recipes in this book with them in our kitchens.
All the recipes are easy to follow on your own and have
been tested with lots of children.

While you are cooking, you can also pick up some good healthy
eating tips. Start eating the right foods now and you will keep good
food habits all your life. Some of these recipes are low in fat and
sugar, but we also believe that it is fine to enjoy a few treats
occasionally – go over the top and try our chocolate cake
which is wickedly delicious. Just one slice though…

Many of the recipes are simple, like Salad Tricolore and
Crispy Rice Choc Cups. Some recipes, like Shepherd's Pie and
Pavlova, are more complicated but will help you to practise and
improve your cookery techniques. We have also included a page
of basic skills to help you, so read all the introductory
pages carefully before you start.

Most of all, have fun with food!

Roz and
Caroline

Kitchen Information

Before you start

★ Put on your apron and tie your hair back if you need to.
★ Wash your hands.
★ Read the recipe. Collect all the ingredients and equipment you need.
★ Check whether you need to turn on the grill or oven.

While you are cooking

★ When you are cooking over heat and taking things out of the oven always wear oven gloves.
★ When using a knife never cut towards your hands.
★ Always cut on a chopping board.
★ Follow the recipe step by step.

When you've finished

★ Don't forget to do the washing up!
★ Put all the ingredients away.
★ Clean all the surfaces with a hot soapy dishcloth.
★ Check you have switched off the oven, rings and grill.

Tips on measuring

How to measure syrup
Warm a metal tablespoon in a mug of hot water. Spoon the syrup from the tin. It should run off easily.

A pinch of salt
When cooks talk about a "pinch" of salt, they mean the amount you can hold between your thumb and your first finger.

Measuring with spoons
When you measure with spoons they should be level rather than heaped. You can buy metric measuring spoons which are easy to use and very accurate.

Be hygienic as you cook

★ Wash your hands before and during cooking.
★ Wash all fruit and vegetables.
★ Always use clean tea towels.
★ Never use the same cloth to wipe the work surface and the floor!
★ Never taste with your fingers.
★ Keep pets out of the kitchen if you can.
★ Germs like warmth, moisture and time to grow and multiply, so give them cold, dry conditions and no time to increase.
★ Try not to keep food warm for more than half an hour.

Managing your fridge

★ Keep it cold (5°C or colder).
★ Never leave the door open longer than necessary.
★ Never put hot or warm food into the fridge.
★ Do not allow raw food (e.g. meat or fish) to touch cooked food or food that is to be eaten without cooking (e.g. salad or cream cakes).

Words cooks use

Beat
Stir ingredients together briskly until smooth and creamy.

Boil
Bring water to boiling point so it bubbles and gives off steam.

Chop
Cut into small even pieces.

Core
Cut out the seeds and central core of vegetables or fruit.

Dissolve
Let a solid ingredient such as gelatine or sugar melt in liquid.

Garnish
Add herbs or salad to decorate a savoury dish.

Knead
Rub bread dough backwards and forwards on a board to make the dough smooth.

Make a well
Form a hole in the middle of a bowl of flour with a spoon.

Marinate
To soak in a marinade of liquids or flavourings, to flavour or tenderize.

Mash
Break up foods until smooth using a fork or potato masher.

Peel
Take off the outer skin of vegetables or fruit with a vegetable peeler or small cook's knife.

Prove
Leave uncooked bread dough to rise a second time before cooking.

Rubbing-in
Rub fat into flour using your thumb and forefinger until the mixture looks like coarse breadcrumbs.

Season
Add salt and pepper to taste.

Shred
Cut into thin strands by slicing a stack of leaves.

Simmer
Keep water hot, so it bubbles gently but does not boil.

Slice
Cut into long pieces or rings, thick or thin.

Soften
Leave butter or cream cheese at room temperature so it will beat more easily.

Stir fry
Cook quickly, ideally in a wok, turning the food constantly so that it is cooked and crisp.

Whisk
Beat with metal whisk to lighten the mixture with air.

Conversion charts

The conversions are not exact equivalents. Never mix metric and imperial measures in a recipe! If you do, the proportions may be wrong.

Solids		Liquids	
15 g	½ oz	15 ml	½ fl oz (1 tablespoon)
25 g	1 oz	30 ml	1 fl oz (2 tablespoons)
40 g	1½ oz	45 ml	1½ fl oz (3 tablespoons)
50 g	2 oz	60 ml	2 fl oz
65 g	2½ oz	75 ml	2 fl oz
75 g	3 oz	90 ml	3 fl oz
100 g	3½ oz	100 ml	3 fl oz
125 g	4 oz	125 ml	4 fl oz
150 g	5 oz	150 ml	5 fl oz (¼ pint)
175 g	6 oz	175 ml	6 fl oz
200 g	7 oz	200 ml	7 fl oz
250 g	8 oz	250 ml	8 fl oz
300 g	10 oz	300 ml	10 fl oz (½ pint)
375 g	12 oz	350 ml	12 fl oz
425 g	14 oz	400 ml	14 fl oz
500 g	1 lb	450 ml	15 fl oz (¾ pint)
		500 ml	18 fl oz
		600 ml	20 fl oz/ (1 pint)

Oven temperatures

Gas Mark	Centigrade	Fahrenheit
¼	110°C	225°F
½	130°C	250°F
1	140°C	275°F
2	150°C	300°F
3	160°C	325°F
4	180°C	350°F
5	190°C	375°F
6	200°C	400°F
7	220°C	425°F
8	230°C	450°F

All ovens are different and cooking times are only a guide. Get into the habit of touching and looking at food to find out if it is properly cooked.

 When you see a red square like this in a recipe, always ask an adult to help you.

Basic Skills

Shortcrust Pastry

Crumbly pastry is hard to handle, but it tastes much nicer once baked than pastry that is wet and easier to handle.

Makes 300 g of pastry

You will need:
200 g plain flour
pinch of salt
30 g lard or vegetable
    shortening
70 g butter or margarine
very cold water

1 Sift the flour with the salt into a mixing bowl. Cut the lard and butter into 1 cm cubes and add to the flour.

2 Rub the fat into the flour with your fingertips. Lift your hands high and drop the fat back into the bowl to trap air.

3 When the mixture looks like coarse breadcrumbs, add 2 to 3 tablespoons of water. You may need to add more.

4 Mix to a firm ball of dough. Wrap the dough completely in clingfilm and chill for 30 minutes before using.

To Chop an Onion

Once they are peeled, onions can be slippery and hard to chop, so use your knife very carefully.

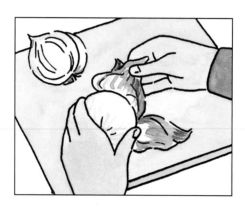

1 Slice the onion lengthwise through the core. Peel both halves. Do not remove the root.

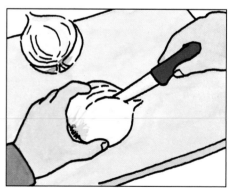

2 Put one half on the chopping board. With a sharp knife make a series of parallel cuts down.

To Separate an Egg

Sometimes you will need just egg yolks or just egg whites for a recipe. This is how you separate one from the other.

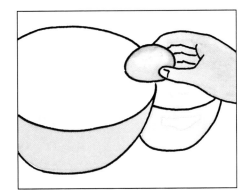

1 You will need 2 clean bowls. Hold the egg in one hand and crack it sharply across the middle against one of the bowls.

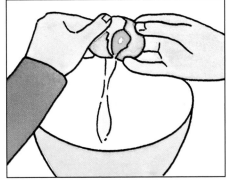

2 Gently pull the shell apart, keeping the yolk in one half and letting the white fall into the bowl.

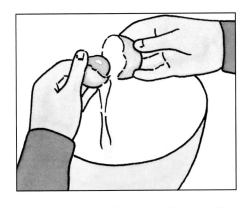

3 Carefully tip the yolk from one half-shell to the other, letting the rest of the white drop into one of the bowls.

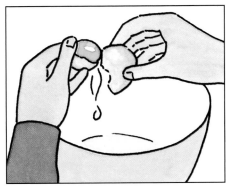

4 Use the broken edge of the empty shell to cut off any white that won't fall. Drop the yolk into the other bowl.

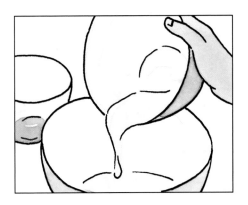

5 If you need to separate more eggs, use two bowls per egg in case you make a mistake, and add them together.

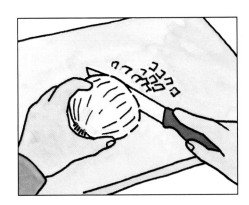

3 Make a series of cuts at right angles to the previous set to chop the onion into little pieces.

To Make Fresh Breadcrumbs

One slice of bread makes about 1 tbsp or 25 g of breadcrumbs. The bread should be about 4 days old. Cut the crusts off and chop finely in a food processor.

To Grate the Zest of Fruit

The zest of an orange or lemon is just the coloured part of the skin. Wash the fruit and grate it on the finest holes of the grater. Take care not to grate the white pith. Be careful of your fingers.

Hamburgers

These hamburgers have lots of flavour and
very little fat. Serve them with any of your
favourite chutneys, ketchups or relishes.

Makes 4 hamburgers

You will need:

500 g lean minced beef
½ teaspoon Worcestershire
   sauce
salt
freshly ground black pepper
TO SERVE:
4 baps, white or wholemeal
salad leaves
tomato and cucumber slices
raw onion slices
chutneys, relish or ketchup

Preheat the grill to a high setting.

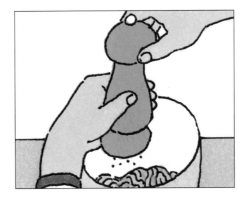

1 Put the minced beef in a mixing bowl. Add the Worcestershire sauce, salt and pepper and mix well with a fork.

2 Shape the meat mixture into 4 equal parts, dipping your hands in cold water. Mould them into flatish rounds.

3 Make a little hollow in the centre of each hamburger. This stops them getting too thick in the middle as they cook.

4 Put the hamburgers on the grill pan and grill for 3 to 5 minutes. Put the baps in the space under the pan to warm.

5 Use oven gloves to lift the grill pan on to a heatproof surface. Turn the hamburgers over with tongs.

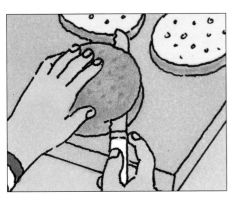

6 Grill again for 3 to 5 minutes. Remove the baps and carefully slit them in half using a bread knife.

7 Remove the grill pan as before. Put the hamburgers in the baps with salad leaves, tomato, cucumber and onion.

8 Serve the hamburgers with your favourite chutneys, relishes, pickles and extra salad if you like.

13

Barbecue Chicken Drumsticks

You can make this Chinese marinade sauce very easily in a food bag. If you use frozen drumsticks, they must be properly thawed.

Serves 4

You will need:
4 chicken drumsticks
2 tablespoons tomato ketchup
2 tablespoons light soy sauce
2 teaspoons clear honey
1 tablespoon sunflower oil
1 tablespoon lemon juice
½ teaspoon Chinese Five Spice
   powder (if you like it!)
TO SERVE:
1 red or yellow pepper
½ cucumber
lettuce leaves

14

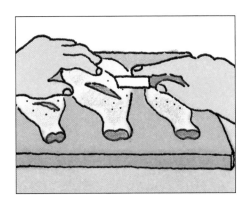 **1** Use a small, sharp kitchen knife to make two or three gashes on top of each of the chicken drumsticks.

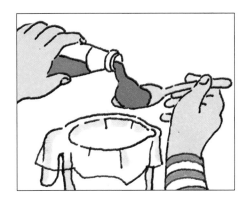 **2** Open a clean, new medium size plastic food bag, put it in a jug and fold down over the sides.

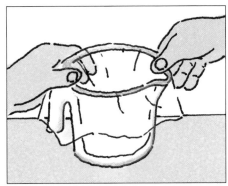 **3** Spoon in the tomato ketchup, soy sauce, honey, oil, lemon juice and spice powder. Twist the top firmly and shake to mix.

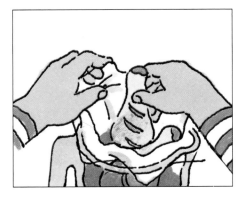 **4** Pop the chicken into the bag. Twist and seal the top tightly with a bag tie. Rub the sauce and chicken together.

 **5** Leave the bag in the fridge for 2 hours. Preheat the grill to high. Put the chicken on the grill pan, and the sauce in a cup.

 **6** Turn the grill down to medium and cook for 5 minutes. Remove the pan and brush on some sauce. Return to the grill.

 **7** After 5 minutes, take the pan out. Turn the chicken using tongs. Brush with more sauce and cook for about 10 minutes.

 **8** Remove the core and seeds from the pepper. Slice the pepper and the cucumber finely. Separate the lettuce leaves.

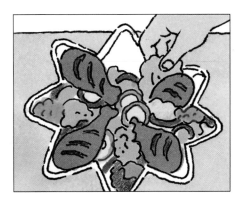 **9** Lay the lettuce on a serving plate with the drumsticks on top and garnish with pepper and cucumber.

Very Special Macaroni Cheese

A creamy, cheesy dish of macaroni makes an ideal weekend lunch, tea or supper. And it can have lots of extra bits added to it to make it more tasty. The all-in-one sauce is very easy to make.

Serves 4

You will need:
1 medium onion
1 small green pepper
150 g mature Cheddar cheese
small packet crisps
salt
1 tablespoon sunflower oil
200 g macaroni
40 g plain flour
40 g butter or margarine
500 ml milk
teaspoon dried herbs
freshly ground black pepper
OPTIONAL EXTRAS:
125 g frozen peas, thawed
6 cherry tomatoes, halved
about 75 g chopped ham

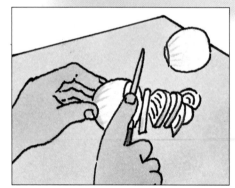

1 Peel the onion, cut in half, then in slices. Cut the pepper in half, remove the stalk, core and seeds and cut into slices.

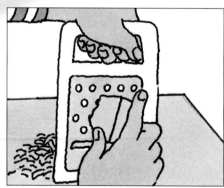

2 Grate the cheese on the coarse side of the grater. Put the grated cheese into a bowl. Scrunch the crisps in the bag.

3 Fill a large saucepan ¾ full of water and bring to the boil. Add a pinch of salt and a tablespoon of oil.

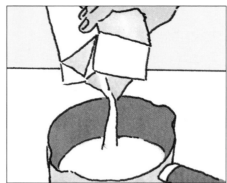

4 Add macaroni, onion and pepper, stir and turn the heat down to medium. Cook, uncovered, for about 12 minutes.

5 Put the flour, butter and milk in a smaller saucepan. Bring slowly to the boil, stirring all the time with a wooden spoon.

6 When the sauce starts to boil, it should have thickened. Turn the heat right down and simmer for about 2 minutes.

7 Take the small saucepan off the heat and put it on a heatproof surface. Stir in the cheese, herbs and seasoning.

8 Stand a colander in the sink and carefully tip in the pasta. Let it drain. Return the pasta to the pan.

9 Pour the sauce into the pasta pan and mix well. Add any extras and spoon into a shallow ovenproof dish.

10 Scatter the crushed crisps evenly over the top of the macaroni cheese. Preheat the grill until it's hot.

11 Place the dish under the grill and wait for the top to turn golden brown. Don't let the crisps burn.

12 Carefully remove the dish from under the grill using oven gloves. Place it on a heatproof surface and serve hot.

Chinese Vegetable Stir Fry

How to love vegetables!

If you don't have a wok, use a large, heavy frying pan. Do all your weighing, chopping and mixing first, so you can cook quickly. The vegetable pieces should all be a similar size.

Serves 3 to 4

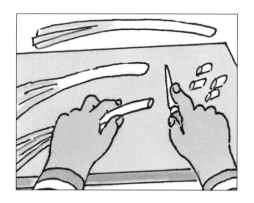

1 Trim the stalk and roots off the onions and cut diagonally into small pieces. Put them into a small bowl.

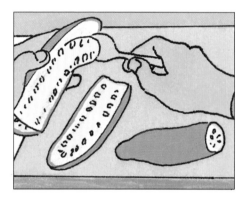

5 Cut the cucumber in half and scrape out the seeds. Cut it diagonally into thin slices. Put them with the peppers.

9 Heat the frying oil, then tip in the onions and garlic. Stir straight away for 30 seconds. Don't let them burn.

2 Peel the clove of garlic and put it into a garlic press. Crush into the onions. You can use a knife to help scrape it off.

3 Cut the pepper in half. Remove the core and seeds and cut it into slices. Put them into another bowl.

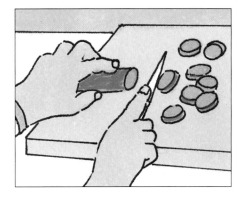

4 Peel the carrots and cut them into quite thin slices. Put the sliced carrot into the bowl with the peppers.

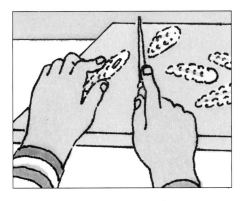

6 Cut the baby corn in half, diagonally too. Yes, these also go into the peppers bowl, with all the other ingredients.

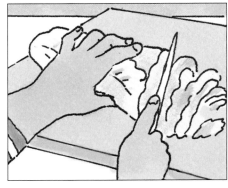

7 Make a stack of the Chinese leaf or crisp lettuce and cut it into shreds. Put these into a separate bowl.

8 Mix all the sauce ingredients – the soy sauce, apple juice, sesame oil and cornflour – in a mug until well blended.

10 Add all the ingredients from the peppers bowl and stir fry these for 2 minutes, stirring most of the time.

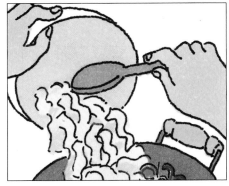

11 Add the shredded leaves to the other ingredients in the pan and stir them for a minute until just wilted.

12 Carefully pour in the sauce, and stir well until thickened and glossy. Serve and eat the stir fry straight away.

Tuna and Pasta Salad

The pasta tastes really delicious if you let it soak in the French dressing. If you don't want to leave it to soak, you may find you need slightly less dressing.

Serves 8

You will need:
salt
1 tablespoon sunflower oil
90–100 g pasta bows
125 ml sunflower oil
3 tablespoons wine vinegar
1 teaspoon French mustard
freshly ground black pepper
432 g can flageolet beans
208 g can red kidney beans
3 spring onions
1 punnet cress
1 small packet fresh chives
198 g can tuna
16 small black olives, pitted
salad leaves to garnish

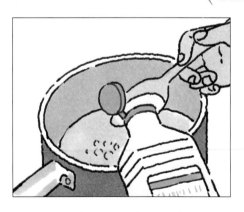

1 Fill a medium size saucepan ¾ full of water. Add a pinch of salt and one tablespoon of oil. Cover and bring to the boil.

2 Carefully remove the lid and tip in the pasta bows. Stir and boil uncovered on a medium heat for 10 to 12 minutes.

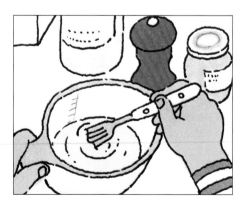

3 Whisk the oil, vinegar and mustard with a fork until the dressing is smooth. Season with salt and pepper.

4 Tip the pasta very carefully into a colander in the sink. Run cold water over the pasta for a minute to cool it.

5 Leave the pasta to drain. Open the cans of beans. Tip them into a sieve over a bowl and let them drain.

6 Rinse away all the cloudy liquid under cold running water. Leave the beans to drain well, then transfer to a bowl.

7 Put the pasta into a large bowl. Add the French dressing, mix well with a wooden spoon and set aside for half an hour.

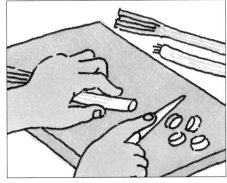

8 Cut the roots and most of the green part off the spring onions. Chop the rest into small pieces. Put them in a bowl.

9 Snip the tops off the cress. Snip the chives into small pieces. Put them all in the bowl with the onions.

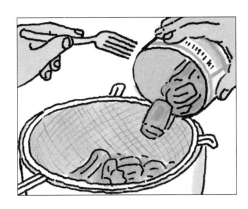

10 Open the can of tuna. Tip it into a sieve over a bowl with a fork and leave it to drain for about 2 minutes.

11 Add the cress, chives, onions, beans and tuna to the pasta. Mix gently. Season with salt and pepper.

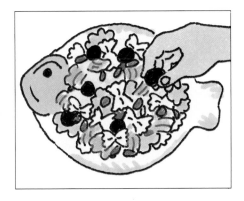

12 Spoon the salad into a serving dish. Scatter with olives, if you are using them, and garnish with salad leaves.

Homemade Bread Rolls

Homemade bread smells delicious when it's baking and it's great fun to make.

Makes 16 rolls

You will need:
1kg white bread flour (or 500 g wholemeal bread flour and 500 g white bread flour, sifted)
2 teaspoons salt
2 sachets easy-blend dried yeast
2 tablespoons sunflower oil
550–600 ml lukewarm water
extra flour, for dusting
extra oil, for brushing
currants

Cottage rolls: *Pull a quarter off each piece and roll both bits into balls. Press the smaller on top and make a hole through the middle with the handle of a wooden spoon.*

Hedgehogs: *Shape the dough into balls. Pull one end out to make a snout. Stick currants on for eyes. Use small scissors to snip the top into peaks.*

1 Mix the flours in a large bowl with the salt and yeast. Make a large well in the centre. Spoon in the oil and pour in almost all the water.

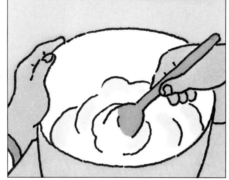

2 Mix the oil and water into the flour with a large wooden spoon until the dough is soft but not sticky. If it's too dry, add a little more water.

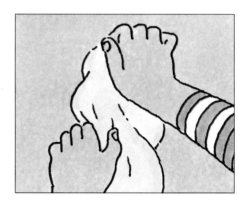

3 Turn the dough on a lightly floured surface to knead. Rub it backwards and forwards with two hands in a scrubbing motion.

7 Leave the dough in a warm place for at least an hour until it has doubled in size and feels spongy.

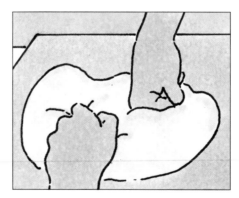

8 Punch the dough down. Knead and turn again as you did before, but only for a minute or two.

9 Cut the dough into 16 pieces. Use some to make cottage rolls, following the instructions at the top of the page.

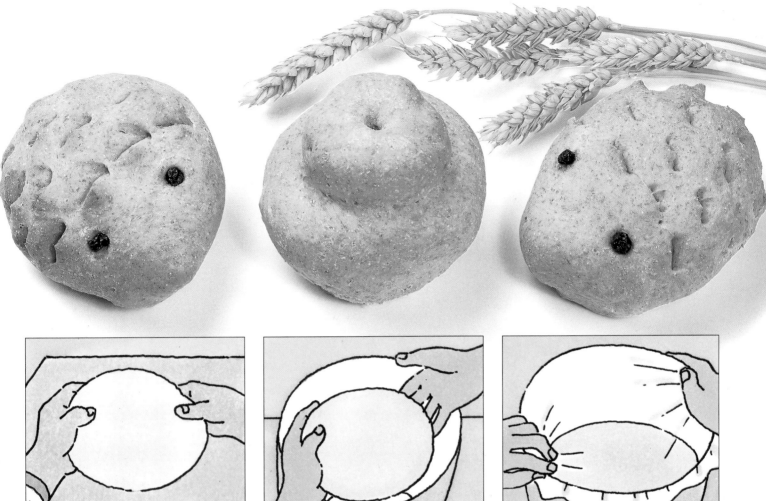

| 4 | Shape the dough into a ball and give it a quarter turn in one direction, either clockwise or anticlockwise. Start the kneading again. | 5 | Keep kneading and turning for 8 to 10 minutes until you have a smooth, springy dough ball. Put it back in the mixing bowl. | 6 | Tear off a large sheet of microwave quality clingfilm to cover the bowl. Brush it lightly with oil, then cover the bowl with it, oiled side down. |

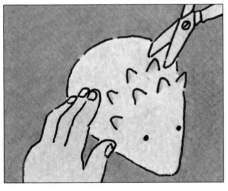
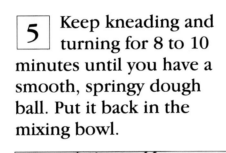

| 10 | Now try following the instructions to make hedgehog rolls. Preheat the oven to Gas Mark 6, 200°C, 400°F. | 11 | Leave the rolls to double in size on a lightly oiled baking sheet. Cover with the clingfilm, but remove it for baking. | 12 | Bake for 12 to 15 minutes near the top of the oven until golden. Remove with oven gloves. Cool on a wire rack. |

Salade Tricolore

Red, white and green are the colours of this simple Mediterranean salad. Serve it with crusty bread to mop up the delicious juices.

Serves 4

You will need:
2 large tomatoes
2 tablespoons olive oil
75 g Mozzarella cheese
12 small fresh basil leaves
sea salt
ground black pepper

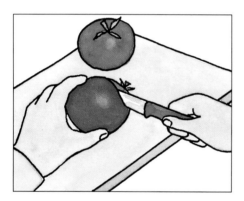

1 Using a serrated knife, slice the tops off the tomatoes as thinly as possible and throw them away.

2 Cut the tomatoes into thin slices and lay them on a round plate, sprinkling in between with salt and pepper.

3 Drizzle half the oil evenly over the tomatoes and tuck some of the fresh basil leaves between the pieces.

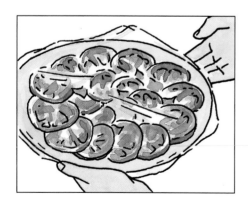

4 Cover with clingfilm and chill in the fridge for 1 to 2 hours, until some juice starts to come out of the tomatoes.

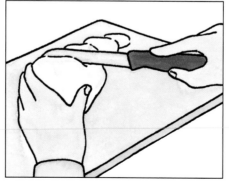

5 Cut the Mozzarella into thin slices with the knife. Uncover the tomatoes and scatter the cheese on top.

6 Trickle over the rest of the oil. Season with more salt and pepper and garnish with the rest of the basil.

Fish Dippers with Tomato Sauce

Make your own fish fingers!

Serves 4

26

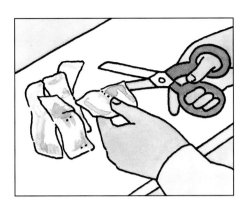

1 Using kitchen scissors, cut the fish into long strips across the grain. Season with salt and pepper.

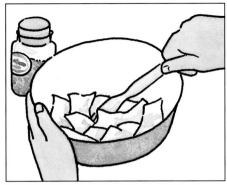

2 Break the egg into a shallow bowl. Add the mixed herbs and beat with a fork. Mix in the fish strips.

3 Put the breadcrumbs and paprika into a plastic food bag. Add 3 or 4 strips of fish and gently shake the bag to coat.

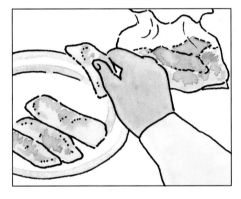

4 Lay the coated strips on a large plate. Repeat with the rest of the fish, just coating a few pieces at a time.

5 Chill the fish in the fridge for about an hour, to "set" the crumbs. Mix the mayonnaise and ketchup together.

6 Heat the oil in a deep frying pan for 3 to 5 minutes. It is hot enough when a cube of bread browns in 30 seconds.

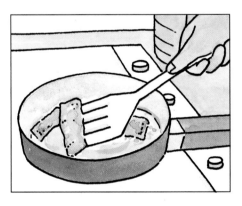

7 Carefully place a few of the strips into the oil with a fish slice. Cook for 2 or 3 minutes, turning once, until golden.

8 Remove with the fish slice and drain on kitchen towels. Fry the rest of the fish, reheating the oil in between.

9 Serve on a plate with the lemon quarters and garnish with parsley. Serve the tomato sauce in a small dish.

Cheese Omelette

Before you make the omelette read the recipe carefully.
Omelettes should be eaten as soon as they are made so you must
be completely organized before you start to cook.

Makes 1 omelette

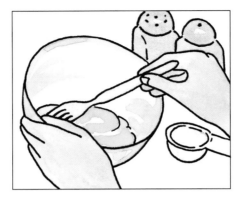

1 Break the eggs into a bowl and whisk lightly with a fork. Mix in the water and salt and pepper to taste.

2 Melt the butter in a heavy frying pan, swirling the butter around to coat the bottom and sides of the pan.

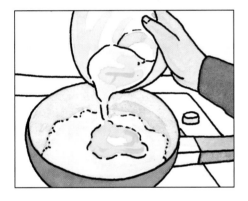

3 When the butter stops foaming, pour the eggs into the pan. Move the pan gently back and forth on the heat.

4 As the mixture sets at the edges, use a fish slice to push the set omelette towards the middle very gently.

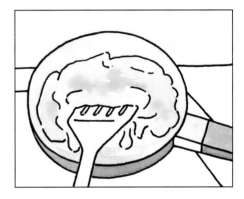

5 At the same time, tilt the pan slightly so that runny egg from the middle replaces the set omelette.

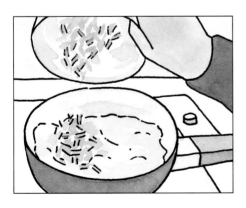

6 When the omelette is set on the bottom but still creamy on the top, sprinkle the grated cheese over one half.

7 With a fork or fish slice fold the half of the omelette not covered with cheese over on to the cheesy side.

8 Carefully lift up the frying pan and slide the omelette on to a plate. Serve immediately, while still hot.

Chicken Satay with Peanut Sauce

Vegetarians can use cubes of tofu instead of chicken. If possible, use wooden satay sticks but remember to soak them in cold water before you start.

Makes 6 kebabs

Warning: contains nuts

30

1 On a chopping board, cut the chicken breasts or tofu into bite size cubes, about 2 cm square.

2 Trim the onions and cut into small pieces. Peel the ginger and grate on the small holes of the grater. Crush in the garlic.

3 Add the rest of the marinade ingredients and mix in the chicken or tofu. Cover and leave in the fridge for 1 hour.

4 Meanwhile, make the sauce. Put the peanut butter, water, soy sauce, sugar and lemon juice into a small saucepan.

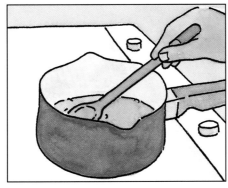

5 Bring to the boil, stirring until smooth. Simmer for 2 minutes and pour into a small serving bowl to cool.

6 Roll the lettuce all together and cut into shreds with a sharp knife. Put it on to a serving plate and leave to one side.

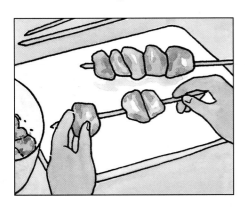

7 Drain the wooden satay sticks if you are using them and thread about 6 pieces of chicken or tofu on to each one.

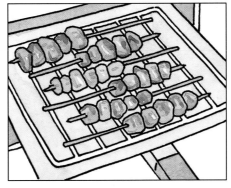

8 Preheat a grill until hot, put the satays under, then turn down to medium. Cook for 5 minutes on each side.

9 Carefully place the satays on the plate lined with shredded lettuce, and serve with the sauce.

Turkey Pilaff

Use the fragrant basmati rice for this dish. It has more natural flavour.

Serves 4

Warning: contains nuts

1 Rinse the rice in a sieve under a cold tap until the water runs clear. Leave the rice to drain over a bowl.

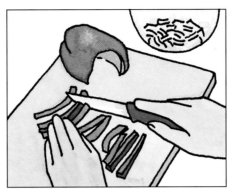

2 Wipe the pepper, halve it, remove the core and shake out the seeds. Cut into strips and then into small pieces.

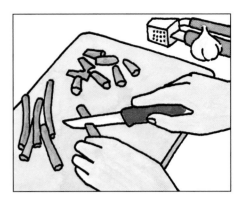

3 Cut the tops and tails off the beans and slice into chunks. Peel the garlic and place ready in a garlic crusher.

4 Heat half the oil in a saucepan and stir fry the meat for 2 minutes. Remove with a slotted spoon, and set aside.

5 Heat the remaining oil in the pan. Add the onion and pepper, then crush in the garlic. Stir and cook for 2 minutes.

6 Carefully add the rice – it might hiss a bit. Stir well and fry gently for about 2 minutes, then mix in the curry powder.

7 Stir in the stock, chutney and beans, then season. Return the meat, bring to the boil, then lower to a simmer.

8 Cover the pan and cook for 10 minutes, then uncover and simmer for 2 minutes. Remove the pan and let it stand.

9 Carefully stir with a fork and taste to check the seasoning. Serve hot, topped with yogurt and toasted almonds.

Vegetable and Bean Hotpot

A great meat-free main meal that is
tasty and wholesome.

Serves 3 to 4

You will need:

2 medium size leeks
2 carrots
I red pepper
125 g button mushrooms
3 tablespoons olive oil
2 tablespoons wholemeal
   flour
400 g can chopped
   tomatoes
150 ml stock or water
432 g can mixed pulses or
   red kidney beans
½ teaspoon dried thyme
2 bay leaves
3 medium size potatoes
25 g butter, melted
salt and pepper

*Preheat the oven to Gas Mark 5,
190°C, 375°F*

1 Trim the leeks, then cut into thick slices. Wash well in a colander. Peel the carrots and cut into slices or sticks.

2 Halve the pepper, remove the core and shake out the seeds, then cut into slices. Cut the mushrooms in half.

4 Stir in the flour, then add the tomatoes, stock and the liquid from the beans. Bring to the boil and add the herbs.

5 Season to taste, simmer for about 5 minutes, then add the beans. Pour into a medium size casserole dish.

6 Peel the potatoes and cut into very thin slices. Arrange these on top of the casserole in overlapping circles.

3 Heat the oil in a large saucepan and fry the leeks, carrots, pepper and mushrooms for about 5 minutes until softened.

7 Brush with melted butter and bake uncovered for an hour, or until the potatoes are golden and crisp.

Shepherd's Pie

This takes quite a long time to make but you can make it one day and reheat it the next.

Serves 4 to 6

You will need:

FOR THE MEAT SAUCE:
650 g lean minced beef
1 tablespoon oil
1 onion, finely chopped (see page 12)
1 carrot, finely chopped
1 stick celery, finely chopped
2 teaspoons flour
300 ml water
1 bay leaf
Worcestershire sauce (if you like it)
1 tablespoon tomato ketchup
salt and pepper
FOR THE MASHED POTATO:
700 g potatoes, peeled
150 ml milk
25 g butter
salt and pepper
15 g extra butter

1 Heat the oil in a frying pan. When it is really hot, add a third of the meat and fry until lightly browned.

2 When the meat is cooked, remove with a slotted spoon and put it in a saucepan. Repeat with the other two thirds.

3 Fry the onion, carrot and celery in the frying pan until soft and brown. Add the vegetables to the mince in the pan.

4 Add the flour to the saucepan and stir well over the heat for one minute. Add the water and bring to the boil.

5 Add the rest of the ingredients and simmer gently for 45 minutes. Add more water if it starts to look dry.

6 Preheat the oven to Gas Mark 6, 200°C, 400°F. Cut the potatoes into even chunks and boil them for 10 to 15 minutes.

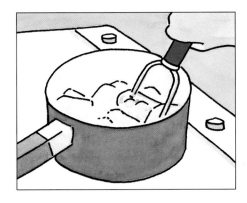

7 Drain the potatoes through a colander in the sink, then return them to the saucepan and mash over a gentle heat.

8 Push the potato to one side of the pan, pour the milk into the other side and heat the milk until it bubbles.

9 When the milk is nearly boiling, add the butter and then beat into the potato. Season to taste with salt and pepper.

10 Remove the bay leaf, then tip the mince into a pie dish. If it is very wet, spoon off some of the gravy. Cool for 10 minutes.

11 Spoon the potato over the mince and spread it flat, making a pattern on top with a fork. Dot with knobs of butter.

12 Using oven gloves, put the pie in the oven and bake for about 45 minutes, until the top is golden brown.

Funny Face Pizzas

Use half the amount of bread dough from the previous page to make your own fun pizzas.

Makes 6 pizzas

You will need:

half the bread dough, prepared to step 8, rolled into 6 balls
sunflower oil, for brushing
397 g can chopped tomatoes
FOR THE FACES:
150 g Mozzarella cheese, sliced for the eyes
button mushrooms for noses
slices of green and yellow pepper
black olives, pitted, for eyes
cherry tomatoes for ties
fresh chives and chicory leaves

Preheat the oven to Gas Mark 6, 200°C, 400°F

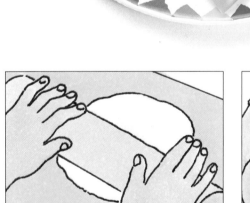

1 On a lightly floured surface, roll each ball into a flat circle, about 15 cm across. Brush lightly with oil and place on an oiled baking sheet.

2 Add chopped tomatoes to each round, then follow the photograph to make faces. You can make up your own ideas if you prefer.

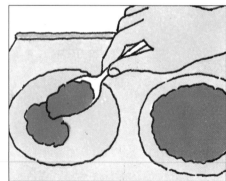

3 Bake for 10 minutes until browned. Remove carefully from the oven and lift on to plates. Add the chicory ears, chive whiskers and tomato tie.

Flapjacks

These biscuits are easy to make and delicious to eat. Be careful when spooning the golden syrup. It can be very messy!

Makes 16

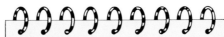

You will need:
150 g butter
1 tablespoon sunflower oil, for greasing
200 g porridge oats
2 tablespoons golden syrup
100 g demerara sugar

Preheat the oven to Gas Mark 5, 190°C, 375°F

1 Melt the butter in a small saucepan. Don't let it go brown. Grease a shallow baking tray, about 30 cm by 25 cm.

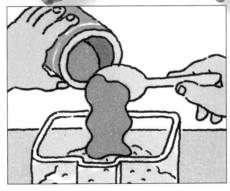

2 When you have weighed out the oats, leave them in the scale pan and spoon on the golden syrup.

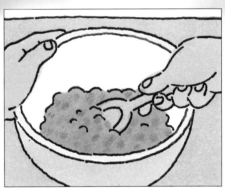

3 Tip the oats and syrup into a bowl. Add the sugar and the melted butter. Mix well with a wooden spoon.

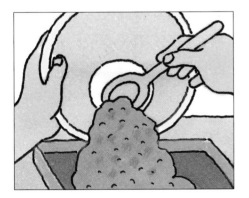

4 Tip the mixture into the greased baking tray and press it down flat with the wooden spoon.

5 Put the tin in the oven and bake for 25 to 30 minutes until golden and brown at the edges.

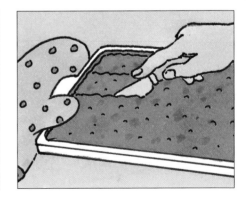

6 Carefully remove the tray using oven gloves. Cut into 16 fingers and leave to cool in the tin.

Crispy Rice Choc Cups

Be careful when you pour the rice pops as they can spill all over the place.

Makes 14 to 16 Choc Cups

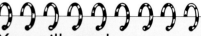
You will need:

50 g deluxe plain chocolate, for cooking

50 g butter

2 tablespoons golden syrup

75 g rice pops

50 g chopped roasted hazelnuts

12 to 16 paper baking cases

TO DECORATE:

small sweets, chocolates or glacé cherries

Warning: contains nuts

1 Break the chocolate into pieces and put it in a large saucepan with the butter and the golden syrup.

2 Put the saucepan over a low heat and stir until you have a smooth, runny melted mixture. Don't let it boil.

3 Take the pan off the heat, put it on a heatproof surface and mix in the rice pops and hazelnuts, stirring well.

4 Leave the chocolate rice mixture to cool for a few minutes and put the paper baking cases into bun tins.

5 Use two spoons to scoop the mixture into the paper cases and pat down well to make neat mounds.

6 While the chocolate is still soft, press on your decorations and leave the crispy rice cakes to set for about two hours.

Creamy Rich Chocolate Cake

Serves 8 to 10

You will need:

oil, for brushing

125 g self-raising flour

25 g cocoa powder

I teaspoon baking powder

150 g soft margarine or butter

150 g caster sugar

I teaspoon vanilla essence

3 eggs

150 g deluxe plain chocolate,
   for cooking

142 ml carton double cream

2 tablespoons raspberry jam

TO DECORATE:

chocolate buttons, sweets or
   edible flowers

*Preheat the oven to Gas Mark 3,
   160°C, 325°F*

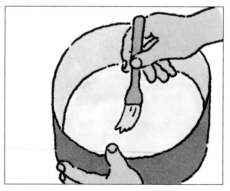

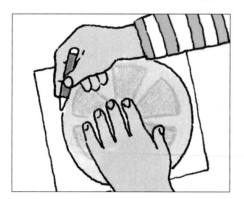

1 Draw round the base of a deep 20 cm cake tin on a sheet of grease-proof paper and cut it out just inside the line.

2 Brush the base and sides of the tin lightly with oil. Press in the paper circle and brush that lightly with oil too.

3 Put the flour, cocoa powder and baking powder into a sieve and shake it into a large mixing bowl.

4 Add the margarine or butter, sugar and vanilla essence. Stand the mixing bowl on a damp cloth to stop it slipping.

5 Break the eggs one by one into a mug, then tip them into the bowl. Add 2 tablespoons of cold water.

6 Beat together well with a large wooden spoon until smooth and creamy. (Use an electric beater if you have one.)

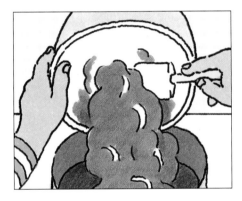

7 Spoon and scrape the mixture into the tin. Smooth the top with a knife and bake in the oven for 40 to 45 minutes.

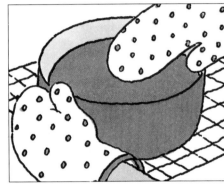

8 Wearing oven gloves, gently press the top of the cake to test it. If it is springy it is cooked. If not, bake for 5 more minutes.

9 Leave the cake to cool for 15 minutes, while you make the icing. Loosen the sides and turn on to a wire rack to cool.

10 Melt the chocolate and cream in a heatproof bowl, placed on a pan of simmering water. Stir well, cool, then chill.

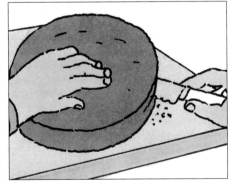

11 Cut the cake in half. Spread the jam on one half and some icing on the other. Put the two halves together.

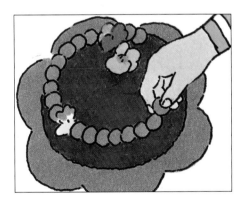

12 Spread the rest of the icing round the sides and on top of the cake. Decorate with chocolates, edible flowers or sweets.

Iced Biscuits

If you make holes in the biscuits, you can tie them up with pretty ribbons.

Makes about 20 biscuits

You will need:
100 g unsalted butter, softened
100 g caster sugar
1 egg
275 g plain flour
2 drops vanilla essence
TO DECORATE:
400 g icing sugar
3 to 4 different food colourings
small sweets, glacé cherries

Preheat the oven to Gas Mark 5, 190°C, 375°F

1 Stand a mixing bowl on a damp cloth to stop it slipping. Beat the butter with a wooden spoon until soft.

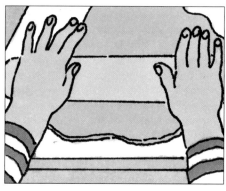

5 Lightly flour a work surface and roll the dough out carefully until it's about as thick as a £1 coin.

9 For the icing, sift the icing sugar into a large bowl. Boil a kettle and pour some hot water into a jug.

44

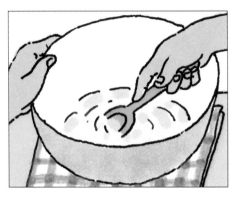

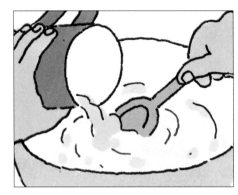

2 Add the sugar to the butter in the bowl and beat again until you have a light and fluffy mixture.

3 Beat the egg in a mug with a fork. Gradually add it to the butter and sugar, beating all the time.

4 Add the flour and just two drops of the vanilla essence. Draw the mixture into a ball with your hands.

6 Use cutters to make shapes and a skewer to make the holes for the ribbons. Lift on to a baking sheet with a fish slice.

7 Bake the biscuits for 8 to 10 minutes until they are brown at the edges. Remove the baking sheet using oven gloves.

8 Leave the biscuits to harden for 2 minutes, then lift on to a wire rack with a fish slice. Leave to cool.

10 Gradually spoon just enough water into the icing sugar to make a soft, firm mixture – about 2 to 3 tablespoons.

11 Divide the icing into 3 to 4 bowls. Add ½ teaspoon of colouring to each one. Wash the spoon each time.

12 Spread on the icing with a table knife. Wash it for each colour. Add ribbons and decorations as you like.

Real Orange Jelly

This is very easy to make as long as you follow the gelatine instructions carefully. The banana gives it a good texture and flavour.

Serves 4

You will need:
5 tablespoons water
2 sachets gelatine
500 ml fresh orange juice
1 banana
TO SERVE:
2 oranges
1 banana

46

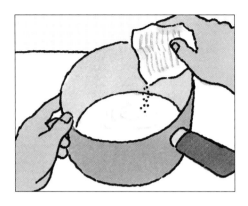

1 Measure the water into a small saucepan and slowly sprinkle the gelatine powder over it.

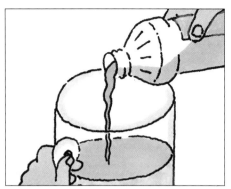

2 Leave the gelatine for 5 minutes until it looks spongy. Pour the orange juice into a large jug.

3 Put the saucepan over a gentle heat until the gelatine dissolves and becomes clear and liquid. Do not stir.

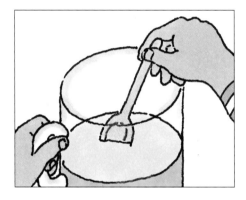

4 When the gelatine is clear and liquid, pour it carefully into the orange juice and stir well to mix it in.

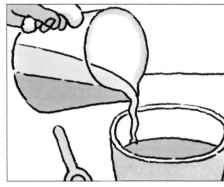

5 Pour half the orange mixture into a serving bowl or jelly mould. Put it in the fridge for about an hour to set.

6 Peel and slice the banana. Arrange it on top of the jelly. Pour over a little more mixture and put it back in the fridge.

7 After about 10 minutes pour on the rest of the mixture and put it back in the fridge for an hour to set.

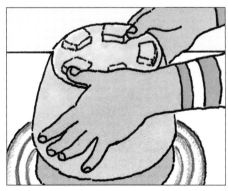

8 To serve, dip the mould into hot water for 10 seconds. Cover it with a wet plate, turn it over and shake down.

9 Remove the mould. Cut the oranges into wedges and slice the bananas. Arrange them around the jelly.

No-bake Lemon Cheesecake

All you need to be good at for this recipe is crushing and mixing. It works best if you leave the cream cheese out of the fridge to soften for two hours before mixing.

Serves 4 to 6

Warning: contains nuts

You will need:
200 g digestive biscuits
100 g butter
1 tablespoon golden syrup
1 lemon, washed
1 sachet gelatine
200 g cream cheese,
    softened
4 tablespoons caster sugar
1 teaspoon vanilla essence
200 g natural fromage frais
150 g natural yogurt
TO DECORATE:
Sliced fruits, nuts or
    chocolates

1 Put the biscuits in a large, thick food bag on a board. Tie the top firmly. Crush them finely with a rolling pin.

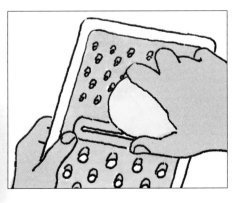

5 Grate the lemon finely into a medium size bowl. Cut the lemon in half and squeeze all the juice on a lemon squeezer.

9 Spoon the cream cheese into a bowl. Add the grated lemon rind, sugar and vanilla essence. Mix well until smooth.

 **2** Melt the butter and syrup in a large saucepan until runny. Put the saucepan on a heatproof surface.

 **3** Stir the crumbs in well, then spread the mixture over the base and up the sides of a 20 cm loose-base flan tin.

 **4** Pat the mixture down well with a metal spoon. It should be cool by now. Chill it in the fridge for about an hour.

 **6** Pour the juice into a mug and sprinkle on the gelatine. Leave it until the gelatine is solid and looks like wet sand.

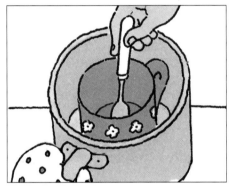 **7** Bring a saucepan ⅓ full of water to a gentle simmer. Carefully stand the mug in the pan and stir the gelatine.

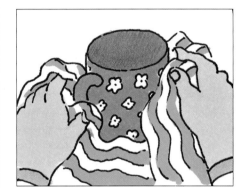 **8** Continue stirring until the gelatine is liquid. Remove the mug with a tea towel and let it cool for 5 minutes.

 **10** When the mixture is smooth, gradually stir in the fromage frais and yogurt, followed by the gelatine.

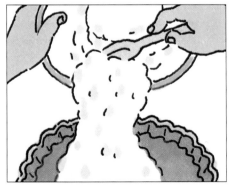 **11** Tip the cheesecake mixture into the flan case and spread it out. Return it to the fridge for 2 to 3 hours to set.

 **12** When it is firm, push up the flan base carefully and slide the cake on to a serving plate. Decorate it as you choose.

Drop Scones

These are really best if you cook them just before you want to eat them.

Makes about 40 scones

You will need:
250 g plain flour
½ teaspoon salt
½ teaspoon bicarbonate of soda
½ teaspoon cream of tartar
300 ml milk
1 egg
2 tablespoons oil, for greasing
TO SERVE:
butter
jam

50

1 Put the flour, salt, bicarbonate of soda and cream of tartar in a sieve over a large mixing bowl. Sift it into the bowl.

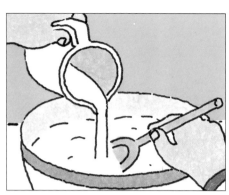

2 Make a well in the middle of the flour with a wooden spoon and add half the milk. Stir to draw in some of the flour.

3 Beat the egg with a fork and trickle it into the flour and milk. Beat the mixture well to make a thick batter.

4 Gradually add more milk until the batter is like double cream. Cover with clingfilm and leave to stand for 10 minutes.

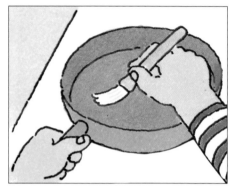

5 Tip the oil into a little dish and use a pastry brush to paint a thin film of oil over the base of a large non-stick frying pan.

6 Heat the frying pan until the heat starts to rise. Drop in a tablespoon of batter. It should sizzle slightly.

7 When holes appear on top of the drop scone turn it over with a non-stick fish slice and cook for another minute.

8 If the first drop scone works well and you have a large pan, you can cook several at once, using a little more oil each time.

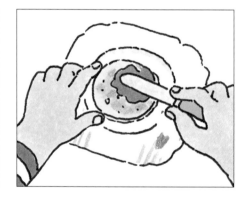

9 Keep the scones warm until you have finished the batter, then serve them with butter and chunky jam.

Easy Breakfast Muffins

You can weigh the ingredients out the night before you plan to have these muffins, then just mix and bake in the morning. Eat them while they are still warm.

Makes 12 muffins

You will need:

200 g self-raising flour

1 teaspoon ground cinnamon

40 g soft brown sugar

50 g raisins or chocolate chips

1 (size 3) egg

250 ml milk

2 tablespoons sunflower oil

12 paper baking cases

Preheat the oven to Gas Mark 5, 190°C, 375°F

1 Put the flour and cinnamon into a sieve, then stir them into a large mixing bowl below to sift out any lumps.

2 Mix in the brown sugar and raisins, or chocolate chips. Break up any lumps in the sugar with your fingertips.

3 Break the egg into a jug and beat it with a fork. Then add the milk and the oil. Beat again until well mixed.

4 When you are ready to bake, put 12 large paper baking cases into a 12 hole bun tin, ideally with deep, straight sides.

5 Quickly stir the two mixtures together but be careful not to overbeat. It doesn't matter if you can still see some flour.

6 Spoon into the paper cases and bake for 15 minutes until risen and brown. Remove from the oven with oven gloves.

Orange Shortbread

Shortbread is particularly delicious if it is
made with ground rice.

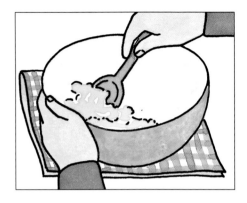

1 Put the butter into a mixing bowl. Stand the bowl on a damp cloth to stop it slipping and beat the butter until soft.

2 Add the orange zest and beat lightly. Add the sugar and beat again until the mixture is very soft and creamy.

3 Sift the flour and ground rice into the bowl and mix quickly but lightly to a smooth paste. Don't worry if it is a bit dry.

4 Place a small flan ring on a baking sheet and press the paste into it. Remove ring and flatten with a rolling pin.

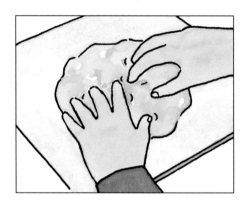

5 If you do not have a flan ring, just press the paste on to a baking sheet and shape it into a 16 cm circle.

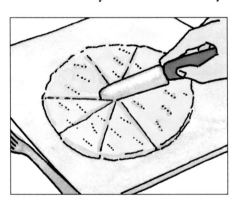

6 Prick lightly with a fork and then mark into 8 wedges with a knife. Sprinkle lightly with a little extra caster sugar.

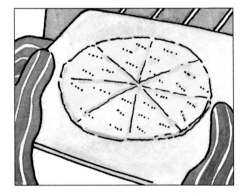

7 Bake in the middle of the oven for 30 to 35 minutes until it is a pale biscuit colour. Leave to cool for 5 minutes.

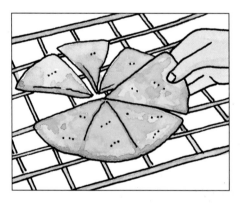

8 Lift the shortbread on to a wire rack to cool completely. When it is cold, carefully break into the marked wedges.

Lemon Cake

This is a deliciously moist cake that is ideal for picnics and lunch boxes.

You will need:
150 g softened butter
150 g caster sugar
2 eggs
grated zest of 1 lemon
  (see page 13)
150 g self-raising flour
4 tablespoons milk
2 tablespoons icing sugar
juice of 1 lemon

*Preheat the oven to Gas Mark 4,
  180°C, 350°F*

1 Put the butter into a mixing bowl. Stand the bowl on a damp cloth to stop it slipping and beat the butter until soft.

2 Add the caster sugar and beat again. Break each egg into a mug, then put them together and beat well with a fork.

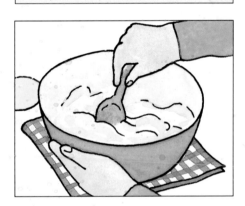

3 Gradually add the beaten eggs to the butter and sugar mixture. Do not add them too fast as the mixture may curdle.

4 Beat in the lemon zest and then sift in the flour. Add enough milk to make the mixture of dropping consistency.

5 Spoon the mixture into a 900 g non-stick loaf tin and spread it flat with a spatula. Bake for 40 minutes.

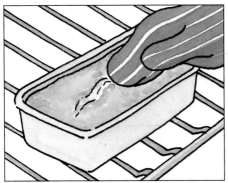

6 Wearing oven gloves, test the top of the cake. If it is springy it is cooked. If not, bake for 5 more minutes.

7 Mix the icing sugar with the lemon juice. Prick the top of the cake with a fork and pour the juice over while still warm.

8 Leave the cake to cool in the tin for 15 minutes then carefully turn it out and leave to cool completely on a wire rack.

Treacle Tart

If making shortcrust pastry takes too long you can buy a 300 g packet of ready made pastry for this recipe.

You will need:
1 quantity shortcrust pastry (see page 12)
flour for dusting
4 tablespoons fresh white breadcrumbs (see page 13)
grated zest and juice of 1 lemon (see page 13)
pinch of ground ginger
a tin of golden syrup

Preheat the oven to Gas Mark 5, 190°C or 375°F

1 Dust the work surface with flour and roll the pastry out. Use short even strokes and turn to stop it sticking.

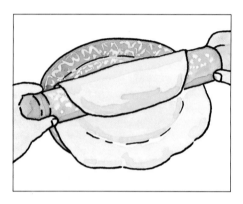

2 When the pastry is big enough to cover a 25 cm pie plate, lift it on to the rolling pin and lay it flat on the plate.

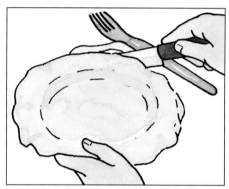

3 Press it into place and cut off any extra pastry. Lightly prick the bottom with a fork but try not to prick right through.

4 Put 8 tablespoons of golden syrup into a saucepan. Add the lemon zest, juice and a pinch of ginger, then heat gently.

5 Pour half the syrup on to the pastry then sprinkle over half the breadcrumbs. Add the rest of the syrup and crumbs.

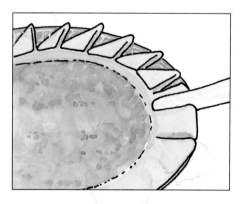

6 Decorate the edge of the pastry by making small cuts all the way round the edge and folding down as illustrated.

7 Put the tart on a baking sheet and bake for 30 minutes until the pastry is golden brown and the filling a little soft.

Pavlova

This is a very easy meringue to make and it tastes lovely if it is still rather soft in the middle.

You will need:
4 egg whites (see page 13)
pinch of salt
200 g caster sugar
1 teaspoon cornflour
1 teaspoon vanilla essence
1 teaspoon lemon juice
142 ml carton double cream
150 g low fat natural yogurt
a mixture of about 500 g of
  your favourite fresh fruits

*Preheat the oven to Gas Mark 1,
140°C or 275°F*

1 Prepare a baking sheet by covering it with a piece of baking parchment or silicone paper.

2 Put the egg whites into a large, very clean, dry mixing bowl and place the bowl on a damp cloth to stop it slipping.

3 Add the salt and using an electric mixer whisk until stiff. Add the sugar gradually, whisking until very stiff.

4 Stir in the cornflour, vanilla essence and lemon juice. Spoon on to the baking sheet and shape into a 3 cm deep circle.

5 Bake the Pavlova for about 1 hour. The meringue is cooked when it looks pale brown and is hard to touch.

6 Remove the baking sheet from the oven and leave the meringue to cool. Peel the paper off when completely cold.

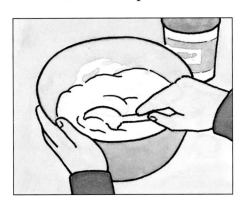

7 Put the cream into a bowl and whisk until thick. Add the yogurt and fold it into the cream with a spoon.

8 Spread the cream and yogurt over the cold meringue and arrange the fruit over the top of the cream.

Variations:
You can use any fruits you like on a Pavlova. We used fresh ripe strawberries, raspberries and plums, but you could try kiwi fruits, mangoes, redcurrants, nectarines or grapes and decorate with mint leaves.

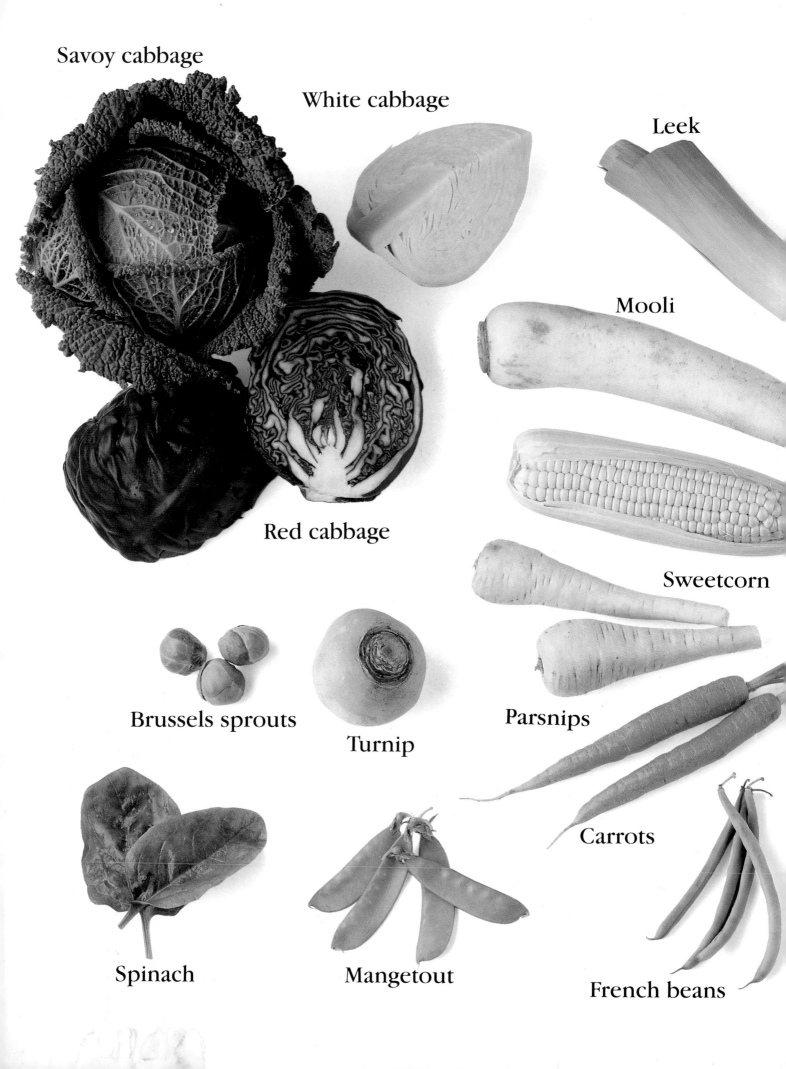

Savoy cabbage

White cabbage

Leek

Mooli

Red cabbage

Sweetcorn

Brussels sprouts

Turnip

Parsnips

Carrots

Spinach

Mangetout

French beans